Water and Life

Nancy Anderson

Rosen Classroom
New York

Water is important.

Water helps things
live and grow.

People need water to live.

Animals need water to live.

Plants need water to grow.

Rain brings water to people.
It brings water to animals.
It brings water to plants, too.

Words to Know

animals

plant

water